G000066923

P

HEART

ACCORDING TO
ST BENEDICT

—

BERNARD DUCRUET, OSB

Translated by Giles Conacher OSB,
monk of Pluscarden Abbey

All booklets are published
thanks to the generosity of the supporters
of the Catholic Truth Society

ISBN 978 1 78469 742 6

Contents

Peace of Heart:
Translator's Introduction

It hardly seems necessary to say so, but peace is the absence of conflict. Paradoxically, we have to struggle for peace in our lives. But peace is a Person, the Prince of Peace, Jesus. In him there is no division, no conflict. His loves are all ordered, he came to do the will of the Father, and he does it. He is the source of our peace. In St John's Gospel (14:27) he tells us, "Peace I give you, my peace I leave you, not as the world gives it. So do not be anxious and afraid." "Peace be with you!", says the risen Christ to his disciples, when they are anxious, worried, trying to understand, to believe. So peace is a gift of the Lord, fruit of his Resurrection – but it comes after his Passion and Death, from the Paschal mystery.

In every Mass, that mystery is renewed; so the Mass is our source of peace. "Peace be with you", says a bishop, as he begins the Mass; "And with your spirit" replies the congregation. So peace is not a one-way traffic: it is a mutual gift, it comes from communion, being in communion with, united to the Church, Christ's Body.

Every Mass we pray "Give peace in our days", because it is a constant need: peace that is the fruit of God's mercy, reconciling us with himself, pacifying the enmity and division brought about by sin. So we ask God to overlook our sins, and to look rather on the Church's faith, and therefore to give peace to the Church, which, being made up of sinners, is constantly rent by divisions. We ask that she be kept from being all stirred up and perturbed, because we are awaiting the blessed Hope, the Coming of our Lord Jesus Christ, when all things will be united in him, when his Lordship over all will be established and conflict will cease, when Peace will be definitive.

But although peace is a gift of God, it is also a task for us. It is all very well to tell world leaders, warring parties, the grasping, envious, or discontented to embrace each other and embrace peace, but that doesn't change much, unless they want to listen. "What's wrong with the world?" asked G.K. Chesterton. He answered, "I am." The only person I can really influence and convert is *me*.

St James points out in his Letter how our unruly desires tempt us and lead us into sin. Jealousy and rivalry, he says, lead to disorder and wicked actions. Peace, mercy and tolerance, on the other hand, allow us to overcome divisions: peace is the seed of righteousness. Wars and conflicts arise from our conflicting instincts, our greed and covetousness. But all this trouble arises from within, from our hearts, where the true battleground is. Our hearts are divided, pulling us one way and another, like corks driven hither and thither by the winds and waves of a stormy sea.

So what we need to do is to establish unity in our hearts, peace; that is what this little book is about. Abbot Bernard lived into his late nineties, helping the monks of his community and very many others outside his community in their efforts to follow Christ, to make him the centre of their lives, so that nothing was dearer to them, so that he could calm their hearts as he calmed the wind and waves for his storm-tossed disciples.

"Pax" is something of a Benedictine trademark, seen everywhere in Benedictine monasteries. My own Abbey of Pluscarden has as its motto a quotation from the Prophet Haggai: "In this place I will give peace." But often you see the word "peace" at the centre of a Crown of Thorns – *pax in spinis*, peace among the thorns, for as Jesus says, his peace is not as the world gives it, where outwardly all is calm and harmony, but in the depths, struggle and division.

"Seek peace and pursue it", says St Benedict in the Prologue to his Rule, quoting Psalm 33, going on, in the course of his Rule, to spell out how to do this in practice. "Not to give a false peace" is one condition: there is to be unity in word, gesture and intent, but hypocrisy breeds trouble. "To make peace before sunset" with the person with whom you are quarrelling, removing division, reestablishing unity. "Everyone will be at peace", he says, if distribution is made according to people's varying needs, and the recipients do not look with proud or envious eyes on what another has received. Guests, since they come in from outside, are to be received with prayer, to be united in themselves and with the community, so that all may be in peace, shown by exchanging a kiss of peace. Peace arising from order is shown in the way the community exchange the kiss of peace according to community order: there is no jostling, struggling, for first place; the tranquillity of order reigns here too. The preservation of charity and peace is a primary concern of St Benedict, and as Abbot Bernard will show, he is alert to every aspect of what needs attention in community life, from humble material matters, to the more complicated human relationships and, finally, to the mystical, directly involving God.

He is down-to-earth and offers practical guidance about the difficulties we face and how to meet them. If we want peace, we have to let our divided hearts be healed, unified, pacified. We need to pray St Faustina's prayer, "Jesus, I trust in You", for in the Gospels we constantly read that Jesus healed all who came to him, and he has not changed. We have only to go to him and invite him into our hearts, to rule in them, to unify them, and peace of heart will be ours.

Giles Conacher OSB

Introduction

Everyone desires peace for themselves, their family, their country, the world. But few are ready to invest in the effort required for the permanent establishment of this peace: "Happy are the peacemakers" (*Mt* 5:9).

Peace is a battle. We are not to submit to the conditions of life in which we find ourselves, but to manage them, so that they become productive of peace. However, at the same time as we are active by trying to establish the conditions most favourable to peace around us, we must constantly accept that peace is a gift of God, which goes beyond all our efforts to bring it about.

This little treatise is not meant to be a theoretical reflection on peace, but a concrete description of the means that a Benedictine community uses – and offers to everyone else – to bring about its motto: *pax*, peace.

Classical literature offers a saying of Cicero as an example of wisdom: "If you want peace, prepare for war".

St Benedict draws his wisdom from the Bible. He quotes the psalm, "Seek peace and pursue it" (*Ps* 33:15).

He directs fraternal life so that it is a continual preparation for peace. "If you want peace, prepare for peace", he seems to be saying to us. Peace is the consequence of taking care to live in the way that he wished and set up, precisely at a time when war was constantly raging in Italy, at the end of the fifth century and the start of the sixth.

From the top of Monte Cassino, where the community had walled itself in for safety, they could see the barbarian armies moving southward, and the Byzantine armies going back up north. One day King Totila himself climbed up to the monastery, on his way to besiege Rome.

So St Benedict was very much preoccupied by this thought of peace when he created this haven of peace in which Romans and barbarians, slaves and free men, literate and illiterate, the sick and the healthy, young and old might live together.

From his Roman temperament and from his Sabine family background, from which came Rome's best administrators, he drew this sense of order and organisation, of which peace is the first fruit. Echoing biblical wisdom, an ancient proverb says: 'Peace is the tranquillity of order' [St Augustine].

In the first part we will discover how peace is fostered by order established among the goods and activities of the community. Then we will see how peace also depends on order established in personal relationships, because charity itself must be ordered. Finally, at a deeper level, we will see how peace is the order established by each of us when we order our passions in our interior life.

However, St Benedict's life itself suggests that there is something beyond this active peace. For at the end of his life he had a revelation of the destruction of his work by the Lombards and the flight of his disciples to take refuge in the city of Rome. Thus he discovered the fragility of every human work, and found peace in a new dimension which is beyond all struggles to bring peace to the earth.

Peace is that gift of God which is above all understanding, and which keeps heart and soul united to those of Christ, opening to us the source of that peace which is beyond trials.

Peace, Ahead of Trials

Peace is the fruit of that order in which a hierarchy of values is established, everyone has their place, the passions are controlled and things themselves are respected. For a young person of our era, that risks looking like a pretty boring world, because people often prefer caprice to structure, spontaneity to order, a passionate life to calmness of soul... But for anyone who wishes to go forward into the adventure of man with God, it is necessary to affirm their nature, to pacify it and to set it in order.

To the novice turning up at the monastery, St Benedict proposes the quest for God and pursuing this by following Christ – that is the chief object of our life. That is why he tries to calm the secondary combats within us, so as to conserve our energy for his service by bringing about a setting of order and peace.

Order in Things

To start with, peace is the fruit of order established in things, order in the things we use. The goods and resources of the monastery are to be respected for what they are. They bring the brothers into communion with one another, through the service they offer, by the sharing they bring about, by the comfort they bring. Things are therefore to be kept and stored away in order.

The one who looks after them is chosen not so much for competence but more especially for his monastic wisdom – in other words, his capacity to discern between, on the one hand, the necessity and usefulness of service rendered to the brethren, and on the other hand, the avarice of an administration which hoards up for itself, for the pleasure of administering, or which collects things in view of their cash value, rather than in view of the service they can offer.

In ancient monasteries they used to build store-rooms and libraries which looked like churches. St Benedict recommends that all objects be respected like the sacred vessels of the altar. For the truth is that every object has the same value – that of bringing the brethren into relationship with each other.

Further, in the monastery there is no pecking-order based on the administration of things. For whenever you set up a hierarchy based on the value of things, you set up a hierarchy of those in charge of them: the banker becomes more important than the peasant, and the oil-producing country more important than the one producing coffee. But the sacristan's job is no more noble than the gardener's.

St Benedict insists that in the monastery's services, you pass things on to the next incumbent tidy, clean and in good condition. We know that a dented car will soon have a second dent, and that no one will know how it got it. In the same way, when the crockery starts to get chipped the contagion of negligence quickly takes hold of a community. St Benedict asks that whoever damages, breaks or destroys something should admit it and ask the community's forgiveness.

It is not the intrinsic value of things which underlies this admission of fault, but the desire to pacify and calm, so that the resentment felt by the brethren, when they discover the clumsiness, the carelessness, the disappearance of a book or the wastefulness, should be immediately forgiven by everyone, so that everyone should be more careful in their use of things.

Distraction, indeed, is always a sign of a lack of paying attention, a lack of watchfulness; and negligence reveals something of a state of mind which, in a community, is not a source of peace, but on the contrary is the source of murmuring and complaints, sometimes justified. But murmuring is the thing most incompatible with peace of heart, and that peace which we should have, spreading out in the community.

Nowadays, on account of having plenty of everything, we have lost some of the respect which we ought to have for everything. Bread has lost the symbolic value which it had in a meal when it was shared: that of establishing communion, in "com-panionship" ["with bread"]. Wasting things is not part of peace. We no longer know that quality of life where everything is respected because things are scarce, and because sharing is vital.

Therefore this sharing of things is also an element of peace, provided it is done with fairness and justice. In community we share according to the needs of each – in other words, taking account of the weakest. But nothing is more difficult to carry out in practice than this kind of sharing, which is not egalitarianism. Here too, discernment and wisdom are needed.

Thus the cellarer [the monastic CEO, responsible among other things for the monastery's material administration] will be rather a humble man, capable of relating well to the abbot, the brethren, the guests and the poor, and with God, rather than being a qualified specialist. He must not make anyone in God's house sad, and must organise his time so as to preserve peace of heart. Then, the brethren who have need of less will rejoice; the others will not be saddened at needing more, nor will they demand as their due what they lack. All will be in peace, if they avoid the murmuring which gives birth to jealousy.

First of all, then, the peace of the community comes through things being in order and shared fairly. Keeping accounts is nowadays a most valuable tool for evaluating that ordered administration. But it is important that neither avarice nor acquisitiveness should drive the administration. Things have to be run so as to render a service, to give to those who have greater need, to bring about communion between the brothers who manage and the brothers who use.

The cellarer ought to be an agent of communion, not just an administrator. St Benedict describes him as a man of relationships; he calls him the "father" of the monastery. He is an agent of peace through his discernment in just sharing.

But in order to be able to share, you need to be able to produce, because lack, penury, excessive poverty are harmful to peace if you cannot give to each what he really needs – just as much as abundance or wasted things lose their meaning as things that unite through sharing.

Nowadays the officials of the monastery have to exercise discernment in resolving another problem which is pivotal to peace: the inflation of needs that go beyond the primary needs of security or subsistence (health, life), to include formation, studies and spiritual needs.

Where do we find true sharing between those who need more and those who content themselves with less? You have constantly to be striking a balance between the values useful to communion and those which more greatly favour the individual.

The Ordering of Relationships

If we go further in our analysis of peace we discover that it comes from the ordering of relationships between the brothers. St Benedict's Rule includes a chapter on community order, on the place and rank in community of each brother in relation to the others. You might find that surprising. Are natural spontaneity and fraternal charity not enough to give each one his place?

If you think that, you are too quick to forget that in the absence of some sort of order, spontaneous parallel hierarchies very often emerge, based on emotional attraction or instinctive repulsion. That is what happens with animals, whether domesticated farmyard animals or, in the wild, troops of monkeys or packs of wolves.

So it is that in Christian communities you quickly discover the natural distinctions of class, race, clan and tribe which exist in the secular city. St Benedict received into his community monks from the nobility and from slavery. Romans were there, and barbarians, the healthy and the sick, young and old.

Into this gathering, in which instinctive relationships might have set up spontaneous hierarchies, he introduced an entirely arbitrary ordering, based on the date of entry into the monastery. In this way, each learned to accept his neighbour whom he had not chosen, and to rise above the secret sympathies and oppositions which might lead a monk spontaneously to seek the company of someone his own age, of his family, tribe or caste, defending the one and avoiding the other, who felt to him like an enemy.

The cenobitic monk learns to rise above his first reactions to his neighbour, reactions based on feelings; and God knows how necessary that may be, if, for example, our neighbour sings badly, constantly fidgets or sneezes at inappropriate moments, and so on. He teaches us to learn the ABC of charity, which is civilised good manners, courtesy, fraternal welcome.

The whole of this section on rank and place in the community speaks to us of that sensitivity in relationships, which is so difficult to acquire for men and women who share their whole lives together, particularly between the old and the young. For, however pleasant we may be when we are not in our own community, in our own surroundings, equally, when at home, we easily become irritable when our wounded feelings are rubbed the wrong way.

This order in relationships is also and especially addressed to those who have some responsibility in the community, of whatever kind. All should remember that they are at the service of the brethren, and not make their authority felt over the others – even if you are only in charge of the shoe-polish and brushes, you can still make this or that brother feel your authority.

St Benedict asks officials first of all to be humble, simply to keep to their place, neither submissive nor assertive. Service at table is not limited to orderly and exact service of the brethren, but is service with the charity of one who welcomes Christ and serves him.

Thus we pray for the weekly servers, so that their service may be carried out with that quality of charity which cannot be attained without God's help. Each week, St Benedict wanted Christ's action of Holy Thursday to be re-enacted, washing the Apostles' feet and asking them to do the same. Through this symbolic action, Christ founded his Church on a hierarchy of service, whose beneficiaries are those in most need.

In exchange, St Benedict asks that the officials' time be respected, so that they might do their work in peace, and that, in the time that is free to them, they may devote themselves to work requiring more concentration, or to their own spiritual reading. In that way, he thinks, no one in the house of God will be worried or saddened.

This ordering of relationships, which fosters a community's peace, is the particular responsibility of the Abbot and Prior. Still more, should they be people of peace and communion. But one condition essential to the peace of any society is taking into account the education of the poorest. "You will always have the poor with you", Jesus said, and there is no Christian community without its poor.

Thus in the ten chapters of the Rule where he deals with the organisation of the community, St Benedict always takes care to draw the attention of the officials to the weaker brethren's work, the strangers welcomed, the children, the old, the sick, those who cannot follow the common standard. In each of these cases you meet Christ, who desired to identify himself with the poor, the stranger, the sick who were visited.

Thus the goal of the Rule is not the formation of an élite, pure and hard, or to encourage competition in virtue, but to give everyone what is needed for all to reach eternal life together.

Mutual help and support is something altogether different from what is needed for a team that needs to get over an obstacle, to successfully climb a mountain or win a race. The weak must necessarily be left out. Here, on the contrary, the relationship of charity, which makes Christ present, helps us advance towards our goal and fosters a peace which is something very different from that of respect for boundaries.

Peace is very difficult to achieve in situations where there is too much emphasis on selection, competition and the formation of élites, who do not consider themselves at the service of the poorest but are driven by the acquisition of a material, intellectual or scientific goal.

St Benedict considers that sharing in service is just as important for building up communion in the community as the sharing of goods. Perhaps today, in a society in which material, scientific and cultural progress take place so rapidly, we have a better grasp of the Church's task: to help the poor to follow [Christ] and to help the more advanced not to forget those who are poorer. The Church's pacifying and prophetic role is to remind everyone that the ultimate goal of humanity is the communion of saints.

Another aspect of mutual support within our communities, which is also a source of communion and peace, is that of fraternal correction.

A peaceful community is necessarily one progressing towards its goal, which is communion. SS John XXIII and Paul VI said that peace is the name for the development of the whole man and of the whole of mankind. Within our communities, progress in charity is the source of peace. But this progress meets difficulties caused by characters, personal failings, errors, sins… A peaceful community is not one in which holiness is obvious, already achieved, impeccable in its morality.

A peaceful community is one in which faults are not hidden, but acknowledged with humour and even tenderness: where errors are pointed out without harshness; where there is accusation of sins without judgement or their being treated as a source of guilt; where the person can move on from where they are, without the need to cover up. The driving force of this pedagogy of peace is forgiveness received and given, through that mercy which demands so much patience, long-suffering, love, humour, joy and mutuality.

For it is very often the case that this brother or that, who has been put right and encouraged to start again, will tomorrow, now strengthened, be the one who in his turn is able to help up the brother who has stopped by the side of the road. Forgiveness is the source of grace because it restores order. That is also why humble confession of sins to a priest and receiving absolution are likewise sources of grace.

Interior Order

After having spoken of the peace brought about by order in things and the peace arising from order among people, I would like to tackle a further dimension of the combat for peace that is, the combat which each of us wages in our own heart so as to restore order, to redirect it in all its faculties. Most of us, most of the time, obey our feelings, our hearts of sense, and do not dwell permanently in the depths of our hearts.

The feeling heart, the heart of sense, is what is moved chiefly by what comes to us from the senses. It deludes itself by thinking that true Life is found in everything that moves, shines, makes a noise, makes us feel, flatters taste and smell. It is drawn by a thousand desires, each of which seeks to grasp the whole of its desire and its attention for a moment.

In the face of this sense-based knowledge, like a moving exploded drawing, there develops a will that is by turns voluntarist or affective, such as current educational trends have too great a tendency to develop, through competition and straining towards success. This hard will is also brittle.

That is why, in the last chapters of the Rule, before talking to us about the will to obey and good zeal, St Benedict puts us on our guard against this aggressive will that seeks to correct faults, or the affective will that seeks to protect or dominate a brother.

This is because this heart of sense is the seat of the passions: fear, sadness, sorrow or joyful feelings. It is not sheltered from temptations: pride, vanity, avarice, sensuality. This heart of sense, then, is not at peace.

The whole teaching of the Rule consists of leading us to discover the deep heart, and to become stable in it. That is where the hidden heart is, where delight, the "wish to love", is found, the loving will that corresponds to grace.

This deep heart, which simultaneously means what is most interior and the freest and most spontaneous, is moved not by sense-knowledge, but by the rational intellect, which is itself under the impulse of the gifts and lights of the Spirit. This knowledge brings about a virtuous and desirous will, which is obedience to God's will.

The fifth chapter of the Rule describes that extraordinary docility of the disciple to the will of God and of his abbot. This monk, stabilised in the depths of his heart, will obey all his brothers (chapter 71) and will be a source of that good zeal and lively fervour described in the 72nd chapter.

Henceforth, the soul truly enlivens the whole mind and heart, instead of being dominated by them. The passions are redirected, the imagination is at the service of action and contemplation, the sentient part is awakened to all that is beautiful, good and true. The whole being is ordered and brought to peace, the body itself shows that tranquillity of order.

So the whole Rule, in its various parts, is intended to teach us to pacify our heart and to dwell in its depths. The watchfulness of humility, obedience, attention to work, silence, the liturgy, all invite us to dwell in our hearts by going beyond the turbulences of feelings and senses. Having been given peace, we shall bring peace to others.

If I can sum up, the peace of our communities has an organisational aspect: its administration and the sharing of goods. It has a moral aspect, that of the right relationships between the brothers, each having his own right place. It has an ascetic aspect, namely the ordering of each one's interior life.

Now, I would like to go on to show that this peace can only be a gift of God, a freely-given grace: this is its mystical aspect.

Peace, Beyond Trials

The first part of this description of peace in our communities might have led you for a moment to think that peace would come at the end of our efforts to achieve it, and that it would be enough for us to seek and pursue it, as one of the psalms says, in order to obtain it.

Then we might think it was the fruit of our conquests. It would be enough to find that ideal place, where things and the environment seemed to follow an untroubled order, such as you find in some desert spots, where the rocks and mountains have stood for millennia in undisturbed silence, where it seems you can almost feel the density of the mystery of Being.

The Benedictine spirit has something in it of Virgil, for whom peace is the fruit of rural life, of regular rhythm, cultivated landscape, regular buildings. That is peace of place, where it would still be possible to found an ideal community where each would be able spontaneously to remain in his place, and would reveal himself to his brethren marked with that urbanity which leads to relationships full of self-control and thoughtfulness, causing no hurt or misunderstanding.

That peace taught the East to bring the interior man to unity, even to perfect equanimity (in other words, equality of soul). With its universal sympathy for the whole of creation, its compassion and kindliness, which are the Buddhist virtues, we would see in each of our brothers the image of peace seen on the face of the meditating Buddha.

So it is not impossible that some people, rather than seeking God, are pursuing this ideal when they knock at the doors of our monasteries, and are surprised to hear from their Novice Master how many hard and harsh things await them.

For we must indeed insist on this existential reality which daily experience will teach us. Peace, like wisdom and every human value, needs to be redeemed. Peace is continually blocked, in us, in our community, in our environment, by sin. It needs Redemption.

Peace and the Cross

Everything human must, one day, be purified by the Cross of Christ, to rediscover its original dimension at the Resurrection. We have indeed to work for peace in the community, since, some day or other, sin, error or stupidity will nullify all our efforts to acquire that peace in an ordered relationship with things, with people, with God.

We know from experience that some relationships are impossible for us, so much do they stir up in us our feelings and emotions; and we need a long experience of feeling how impossible it is to love an enemy – the brother who "winds me up" and takes over the whole of my life, not letting me live – in order to realise just how much peace of heart is a great gift of God.

Our communities, which are schools of peace, are from time to time tried by the consequences of the sin of the world, by others' sins and our own.

Sometimes trials come from outside: fires, revolutions, expulsions, wars, invasions.... St Benedict learned in advance, in a vision, the fate that lay in store for his monastery, invaded, pillaged and destroyed by the Lombards. At Saint-Benoît-sur-Loire, the monks have had to rebuild their monastery nine times in twelve centuries.

Sometimes trials arrive from the sins of monks who stir up divisions, schism, disunities, murmuring and complaint, or separations.

On Mount Athos, the monastery of Pantaleimon had more than twelve hundred monks at the beginning of the twentieth century. In 1984 it presented the sad sight of its ruins, in which about ten old monks were living. Years of theological disputes had emptied the monastery of some eight hundred monks, during the very time of Staretz Silouan. He charitably scarcely mentions this trial. The last few monks were stirred to action: today forty monks from Russia have come to raise up the ruins.

Sometimes, in a still more mysterious way, the Holy Spirit shakes up a peaceful community to launch it into the adventure of foundations or renewals, giving a new fervour to its peace: that of the Cross. The Gospel confirms us in this paradox: "Do you think I have come to bring peace to the world? No, I tell you, but rather division". (*Lk* 12:51).

It is not possible to be faithful to the Gospel without being faced with this mystery of impossible peace. Wisdom and peace, then, are tried by the consequences of man's sin. They have need of being redeemed by the Paschal mystery. Peace remains a battle which must face all the forces of evil.

Any discipline which offers us peace through human efforts alone, in a programme of asceticism, altruism, beguiling generosity, but paying no attention to the paschal grace of the Christian mystery, is a lying discipline or religion. For whoever says he is without sin makes God a liar. The peace which the sacraments give is indeed a peace redeemed by the Cross. From now on, following Christ, we are in the heart of the way of peace which is a central itinerary in the Rule of St Benedict. Peace is tried and tested....

The Trials of Peace

I would like to sum up with three typical kinds of trial, which every human being and every community experiences at some stage in life. These are the trials of loneliness, the absurd, and death.

The Trial of Solitude

The trial of loneliness confronts us all, some day or other, in our desire for communion, but facing the impossibility of communicating at depth by means of our own resources, our own initiatives.

We are fundamentally beings of communion. However, we are all wounded, and these wounds leave behind heart-breaking obstacles to love. Sometimes from our earliest infancy, we have been suffering from not being properly loved and not having been able to love. That is the first obstacle to peace of heart.

The Trial of the Absurd

Then, some day, we will face the trial of the absurd. It will happen on the day when we begin to realise that it is impossible for us to understand all that is going on and that it is beyond our reasoning mind, that it seems irrational.

It might be something that happens, someone's behaviour, or a metaphysical problem. Whatever it may be, we are faced with a painful choice between revolting against the absurdity of the thing, or embracing the mystery. It requires a complete conversion of our understanding.

The Trial of Death

Death, ultimately, sums up all the trials that we at some stage encounter, even every day, by revealing the limits of this mortal life. Old age or sickness, failure or accident, hunger or thirst set before us the sorry reality of our limitations, striking at the life-energy in which we put our trust.

Then we find ourselves doubting ourselves, others, and everything else on which we like to rely. A kind of non-existence presents itself to us, whose drama is set constantly before us by philosophers and novelists.

How to Live Through Trials

Trials, whether of loneliness, absurdity or death, cause us to lose the peace of mind which we had so long sought and built up in our relationships with others, with things and in the pacification of our own hearts.

In community or in our personal life, we need to discover the reality of that experience, when peace now seems to have totally fled our lives, whether through external conflicts or interior trials that plunge us into the anguish of loneliness, absurdity and meaninglessness, or death.

The Wisdom of the Cross

The wisdom of the Cross demands that we avoid false sufferings, those arising from the worsening of our trials which we, consciously or unconsciously, cause ourselves; above all, it demands that we go through the real trial with which following Christ presents us. We will then rediscover peace, but only after the trial.

For that to happen, we need to accept and enter into the trial, whether of loneliness, absurdity or death, without hardening or armouring ourselves against it so as to be unaffected by it; without revolting against it in order to overcome the suffering; without fleeing, being well aware that the trial is within us, and we will encounter it again elsewhere.

It is also good not to over-dramatise it (but we should equally avoid minimising it). Much of the worsening of sufferings and trials arises from our wrong attitudes to them.

We need to be realists. We will not find peace other than in the trial itself, by agreeing to follow Christ on his way of the Cross. That peace will be found redeemed and transfigured by the gift of life beyond death, the fruit of trust and self-abandonment.

For Christ did not make use of the power which was his in his divine nature in order to avoid suffering and save himself from the trial of the Cross. He went to the very end of the loneliness of abandonment.

He experienced to the limit the absurdity of the situation of the condemned innocent, the creator accused by the creature. He went all the way to death, all the way to his last breath. He consented to the trial which was put before him, in trust and abandon, waiting on God alone, to be saved from death, beyond death, by the Resurrection.

In our trials it is good for us to meditate on the Passion of the Lord. It is just when we offer him our crosses, by detaching ourselves from them, and when we take up his

Cross, that we discover how much his Cross is carrying us, because it is life-giving and glorious, while ours crush us.

Abandonment

I would like to develop a little more the meaning of this path of self-abandonment which we have to follow in our trials. Three words sum up this attitude of "active abandonment": welcoming, consenting, offering.

Welcoming

First of all we need to welcome realistically the trial that is set before us, to see it in the full light of day, standing back from it, so as neither to dramatise it nor to hide or minimise any aspect of it. It involves an effort to be lucid about it, so that we can get away from reactions limited to our feelings.

Just to face up to the trial I am asked to live, or the temptation that has seized me, or, again, the precise nature of the order I have received, but which seems to me impossible, already requires a great grace of strength.

For that I need to rid the trial of all the elements which my imagination adds on to it. But the light or lucidity which I must bring to this first stage will impact on my own subjectivity and my attitude in the face of this trial.

I shall need to face up to the revolt I am feeling, the fear which invades me, the sadness which paralyses me, the sorrow which prevents me from thinking or reacting. In short, I will take account of all that goes along with my trial, in my feelings, in my emotions, in my imagination. That is what welcoming the trial realistically means.

But it is good to perform this enlightened acceptance of the trial with a brother or spiritual father who can help me to take the precise measure of the effort it demands, to calm everything which the imagination uselessly adds on to the trial, or to see what element of my trial arises from injured vanity, humiliated pride, deprived feelings… because all that is bad suffering, which I can pacify by pacifying my passions, with God's grace.

Freedom must grow in me, and freed from the passions I will be in a better state to deal with the objective trial, with the strength that comes from the Cross.

But in the light I will perhaps discover, to my great confusion, that there is no objective trial, that the combat is purely one of the feelings… It is most important to have seen this and realistically to accept my weakness.

So already, in this first stage of light, I will find a great peace.

Consenting

The second stage of this path of abandonment, once the spirit is calm, says St Benedict, is to embrace patience – in other words, to enter into this trial with the sweetness of consent.

Consenting without flight, without armouring ourselves against it, without stiffening up, without rebelling against it. Consenting to the absurdity and meaninglessness which I do not understand, consenting to loneliness of heart, consenting to the sorrow of the little or great death which it has been given me to live.

Consenting also means feeling: feeling in my senses, in my imagination, not rejecting anything out of fear… Embracing harsh circumstances and wounding injustices.

Consenting to be tried for as long as God wishes. Consenting to wait for God and his time, as St Benedict says. Bearing and enduring for the Lord, on account of him. So, as we consent, we will discover the joy of victory, a strength like Mary's, which supported her at the foot of the Cross, and which is already a sharing in the new life that will flood into us completely at the Resurrection.

What the Lord asks of us, when we are a bit wiped out by the trial, is to believe God, to hope in him, because he is just as Almighty as he is God. To hope, even when we are flat on our faces, incapable of getting up, but to hope with a lively, indestructible hope. In those moments we do not recognise the Cross in the suffering which seems like a monstrous contradiction; it is only afterwards that we come to realise that through that suffering, that temptation, we have become what we are.

Madeleine Delbrêl

Offering

Lastly, we distinguish a third stage in this movement of abandonment to God's will, though of course, in real life, these three stages form a single leap of the soul. This third stage is that of offering: "For you, on your account, we are condemned to death all day" (*Ps* 43:23).

This offering, this cry to God from out of the depths of our trial, this opening to what is above, has the power to overturn that attitude of withdrawing into wounded nature, mortified vanity, disappointed pride, deprived sensitivity, and to rediscover an attitude of offering, open to the mystery and not brought up short by the absurd or closed up in loneliness.

This attitude of trust and faith in love is the essence of the spiritual sacrifice which is asked of us. Then we no longer identify ourselves with the trial, the suffering, the temptation. We give ourselves over completely to God in a surge of love. By charity, entrusting himself to God's help, the monk obeys in what seems impossible to him (see chapter 68 of the Rule).

This is when a new dimension of peace and joy is born, and then begins to grow in the heart of the trial. A new life that is very humble, unforeseen, tender. Joy which endures in the trial. Life flowing from the pierced Heart of Jesus, first-fruits of the Resurrection. Presence of the strength of the Holy Spirit.

This peace which comes from God has no limits. The human peace which we were initially seeking was limited by all sorts of rules, boundaries arising from the place assigned to each thing and to each person, and which, even if they are accepted, are inevitably limiting.

The peace of God is limitless, even to the extent of sometimes frightening us a little. It is so hard for us to detach ourselves from our limits…

May the peace of God which is beyond all understanding guard your hearts and thoughts in Christ Jesus.

Conclusion

We can conclude these reflections on peace with two testimonies, one by Patriarch Athenagoras, and the other an anonymous prayer, written in Yiddish, discovered in the camp of Auschwitz-Birkenau.

It is necessary to wage the most unrelenting war against oneself, until we have been disarmed.

I have fought this war for years; it has been awful. But now I have been disarmed.

I no longer fear anything: love drives out fear. I am disarmed of the desire to be right, to justify myself by disqualifying others. I am no longer on my guard, jealously clutching my riches. I welcome and I share. I do not strongly hold on to my own ideas, my plans. If someone comes up with something better – or rather, not better, just good – I accept that without any regret. I have given up comparing. Whatever is good, true, real, is always better for me. That is why I am no longer afraid. If you disarm yourself, if you dispossess yourself, if you open yourself to the God-Man who makes all things new, to Him, He wipes away the bad past and gives us a new age in which everything is possible.

Patriarch Athenagoras

O our eternal God, blessed art Thou.

Let all vengeance cease, every call for punishment and retribution. The crimes have gone beyond all measure, all comprehension. There are too many martyrs.... So do not measure their sufferings in the scale of your justice, Lord; do not lay these sufferings to the account of the executioners in order to extort from them payment of a terrible bill. Let them be paid back in another way.

To the credit side of the executioners, the denouncers, the traitors, all those men of ill will, set the courage and spiritual strength of the others, their humility, their dignity, their constant interior struggle and their unconquerable hope, the smile that stopped the tears, their love, their broken hearts that remained firm and trusting even in the face of death, yes, even in the moments of greatest weakness.

May all that be set before you, O Lord, for the forgiveness of sins, a ransom for the triumph of justice: may the good be taken into account, and not the evil!

May we remain in the memories of our enemies not as their victims, not like a nightmare, not as spectres that dog their steps, but as supporters in their struggle to destroy the fury of their criminal passions. We ask nothing more of them.

And when all this is over, grant that we may live together, as men among men, and may peace come back to our poor earth.

Peace for men of good will and for all the others.

Anonymous